^{on}words & ^{up}words

Anamaría Crowe Serrano

*on*words

&

*up*words

Shearsman Books

Published in the United Kingdom in 2016 by
Shearsman Books Ltd
50 Westons Hill Drive
Emersons Green
BRISTOL
BS16 7DF

Shearsman Books Ltd Registered Office
30—31 St. James Place, Mangotsfield, Bristol BS16 9JB
(this address not for correspondence)

www.shearsman.com

ISBN 978-1-84861-457-4

Contents

for Mark

Claro está, Platero, que tú no eres un burro en el sentido vulgar de la palabra, ni con arreglo a la definición del *Diccionario de la Academia Española*. Lo eres, sí, como yo lo sé y lo entiendo. Tú tienes tu idioma y no el mío, como no tengo yo el de la rosa ni ésta el del ruiseñor.

Juan Ramón Jiménez, *Platero y yo*

I

frontiers

words falling apart   the legs of broken branches   no simile or
similitude   no language   a rebellion of phonemes biding their
time in the confines of structure   the confines of *your space or mine*
hoping there will be another place

     a past   /tense   preferably more relaxed   what is the word for
future   the word for

                  word   for

             darkness that does not exist

words hold you back   whereas objects breach your border
you look under your skin for an explanation   sometimes there's
i.d.   a pen   a sugar sachet surreptitiously sneaked into your pocket
other debris   but the lights are out and there's a smell of must   a
line you must not cross   femicide   human sacrifice   a line
beyond which

            you are dust and few care

colour clings to you   as a safeguard   seven waves of the spectrum
translated as *who you are*   short wave/long   and that might be
who you are   someone patterned   oblong in the plural   the
gama of colours disperses   is not good enough   you shrink
to an idea   fumbling with consciousness   absence
                       being

       the destination you were aiming for is within and without
reach   like trying to become a crustacean   or a chimney pot
on one level yes   multiple other levels lack stability

       what's the word for reaching your dream but when you get
there it's unrecognisable   arrived-arrivederci   you will never know if
you made it   crossed the border   or if this is a phase   a phrase

that includes the concept of reaching
                    there's always the sniggering doubt that the frontier
beyond which you cannot go and behind which you cannot stay
              contains all of your dna

up the hill

up the hill stars point pentagonal

in a language of their own   so you say

though I'm lost in minor variations of jasmine

lady of the night   distracted

          by mythologies in the sky

ursa could be prowling in the shadows

cicadas screaming in her throat

and I'd never know   not unless

you spelled it out for me

                    I can only hear the gliss

of air along the road   Orion

breathing as he draws his sword

heroic   the why rippling

towards Cadiz   eventually

he'll hit true north leaving a hole

          where meaning

                    was

an elephant

I don't remember holding your hand
or being held   love becomes
some yardstick that warrants
standards shouting screaming threats

your face red peony puffed and frenzied
blowing a blizzard through
this house of straw this house of fear
wrong answers snowballed stuttering

in the old cortina rumbley radio talk fills
the hour's ride home fills the sky
the trees the sun anywhere the eye
will wander melting into tar on summer roads
fills the water shortage and the terror
of my tartan skirt my hideous home-knit
cardigan uncool and fat the grief of error
stuffy   fills the smell of sweat
the stench of conversation strangled in my throat

back home I hide behind the silver knives and forks
drown in their mr/mrs fiction dancing on the table
set with flowers and candles   napkins
and my head freefalling
through barbed comment and contempt
crash landing   sustaining
minor injuries   I shortfall

stonewall the silence, murderous air

spoon packet mash and meatballs

some impoverished sense

of self   recede and shrink

chewing quietly chewing   no god comes

no good or meaning   just the words

forced sweet amidst the mockery

words of grace and blessing good

virtuous words robust sound pillars bastions

of failure   farce   amen

all the truths invisible

as that enormous elephant still lingering over there

in the middle of the room

the stress clinic

it's ok   no one need know   only negligible
impending threat   i'm going to leave you
        let healing happen
i'm turning left into the coffee shop   it's easy
        like this   one step
                                one more
comforting to sit
        even on seats slashed by spooks

i can wait   learn patience is learnt on the edge
        other worlds where others wait
for the breath   something that "presents"
        a hiatus between one distress and
the nest you're reluctant to leave

it's ok   the world is out there   still   the density
you love suspended in space   preparing
the next problem for you to solve   you're good
at that   talented
        are you ok?   me too   it's just
the acid sprung on a tensile in my stomach

without

without

       reading   because words make no sense

           wanting

               everything

all at once so it stays   blistering   with the sting

of 5 a.m. through my eyes   through the bullet hole

          in your bedroom wall

my head is empty

           a pot   punctured

           wanting away again from your fire

my shell is slouched

           towards

             this chair   wood

where a painter's hand articulated age

took the shape of implements   horse-hair

     scraping the retina

with

       irony   pity   his joints swollen

deaf   like my tongue when i bite it

bite it and you perfect the art of *no no no*

your mind working

          over

            time

Booterstown

there I am
in the bend
of a swan's neck

under it
arching towards
limbo mud ballet

a nerve
stretched taut
across the marsh

muscle molecule
ready to rip
the tension of water

vertebrae
twisted between the bars
of trolleys

dumped in the cold
and the silt
patiently gaping

at syllables
the mutterings
of a cloud

my mind's eye
walled
as the train pulls away

mirRor, mirror

they're sending me away to the edge   thinking somethingg will
be learNt   but the the Mind is unyielding a LOCKED door 2
the kingdumb of attention   there's little 2 cling 2   I
lOng for long grass   open hiDing ground☺   not
deskschairsbreezeblockwalls painted *future* grey fuZZZ not the smell
of dbrain cells storming   trickers for

panic☹

me, the emperor **NAKEd** at the thin enD of the eDge

wondering what? next   what next? has been explaineD and I

should! know   every1 nose   But that door is Bolted 2

wood is *stubborn* once it's choppeD   forgets it's

purpose   INSTRUCTION with its iron **fists** keeps knokking but

the logic of **SIMPLE SEQUENCES** is untranslatable

I'm already triPPing before the litany begins!?
e) finally
c) and when that's done
j) an echo
b) Firstly
d) the aim
a) next (surely not again)
e) thirdly, but before you do that

pretending i Don't really want 2 scream!!   my teeth *sink* in2 my jaw
fun is The 1st and last hurDle   the ze-bra on my t-shirt will hiDe my
terror ddistract someone   And my skin will tempeR the tenshun of
every muscle   NO 1 will know? I'm not ALL here weirD
dehinb these stripes   some of me   the bit no 1 sees spiralling in2 a
crater   i fOllOw   keep falling   my face gRows flaTTer
there's despair carveD down my cheek   LOSER :-P tattooed on the
insiDes of my eyelidbs

the polish language

not to understand   to be
inside a sound with no meaning
ignoring help   the time
of the concert   platforms for
unpronounceable places but relishing
the acoustic   somehow handsome
humming the pedal note for structure
noting clusters   cobbled colour
till your tongue is truly gilded
across a line of latitude
unscrambling those infernal eggs

                              behind you
the shop assistant whispers something
that must be about you   the very thing
you were not meant to hear   or understand
pariah or deaf or gone in the head (maybe
foreign) but the gist you get
give it gas he says encouragingly and you nearly
laugh it's so alien in the medieval market

not to know how   in the end/finally/at last
so much of this   not just
cooking or riding a bicycle but physical
ache   my head paining where eptitude should be
the *in* or *ex* or *un* comingling in the negative
        you could knock me down with
a perfective if you knew how   come/

go/ go back/ return/ leave/ depart

nuance   much as the undoing

of the buttons on your shirt or swimming

one arm over the other and under and

dragging the weight of water and over   *could you*

please repeat?   after all those years

of training   fishlike

            to can   innately

not long a few words of able

a string for the wisdom of a sentence

on the blackboard and my notebook

deserving of raindrops

clap clap thunderous electric

praise for the working parts   robotish

I am abling better every day   still, a phrase

and a response from the woman in the cake shop

little being much   [temporal phrase in first

position] slavishly

            slavic knocks down the wall

everything is incomprehension, like Berlin, north-south

just pieces of an ignorance

but now are fine lines the borders

now I speak-tell-say?

            somewhere

the town is opening all its gates   trams

criss-cross a synapse   degrees of politeness

sink in   madam, she says   your phone fell (has fallen?)

and sure enough it's where it shouldn't be

            on the ground

biblos

the library
is full of shelves
sliding into spark
and bacon

you gloss the destinations
lodge snugly
in pergamine ellipsis
an open bracket
to these antique
Dutch illuminations

some glitter so now
blinkety bling con
textbones glowing
glowering at the deficit
of content

you fly beneath the page
because real depth beckons
rowing its draft
your direction
lostbody rescued
by the coldplay of words
on patrol

you can dominate the dream
the expectation
of a safe bookshore
by downloading
a catchy phrase
reissue it for as long as it takes
to find a new exit cum
entry by newby

activate the senses realtime
characters, emoticons
an entire web of recognition
fathering technique
mothering production
ideas you always had
ever so slightly
                    transected

the word modulated, trans-
verse on the verso
all its cities collapsing
on your shelves
arguing hidden points
with artaud, hindered
by a hundred fragments
alluding to the shape
of a thought

that might reshape
thought

once the books rebelled
when you took your eye off them
for a moment
          you didn't even notice
          did you?
guerilla bookfare
broke out

it's still here, its legacy
all around you
issuing a fatwa on unread tomes
virulent, spreading
readying for execution
words globally swarming
storming the place

their essence
materialises with dragonforce
it can salvage the craft
as it paddles towards you, amused
at having survived
the war, after all
the shelling of structure

there's no accounting
for rime nor reason

foreign influences
meridional traditions
packing your shelves

and you floundering
at the foot of the mountain
still searching for a foothold

(in the beginning)

you

stood obscured at the top of the stairs troubling through me

in the dark   -cryptic-   it's how I remember particular particles

of your face

lights out because of the solar flare

what it does to the power grids

back then it was the aurora borealis ahead of you   oceans mountains gorges

wild flowers snow

versus state exams   the loss that comes with choice and other

promises to yourself that you'll have to fill in for yourself

your eyes unbelieving in their sleepwalk as if coronal mass would stop still

not quicken your mantle or cling to your pyjama buttons   the only thing

missing was a fluffy toy folding from your hand to cliché that frame

the need for props

always at the core like yesterday   rabbited again in headlights

combatted by finesse   overload   falling into space

panic is another of your histories and   in the end   this is

just another beginning

you

lighting the northern moods with paper

butterflies pasted

on the bedroom wall   pink yellow blue   and tadpoles rescued

from the lab

Obituary

i.m. Anne Leahy

it can happen any day
that you drop in
larger than life, beaming
the silence vociferously past me

but I have no stops to pull
that might change a thing
not a one
– my fingers are numb –
just a hunger for the freshness
of your skin
the lustre of your hair
a sentence half-begun
stuck in the broken circuitry
of a life that fell
just short
of opportunity

the organ booms cancrous
'round the vaults
and you play it wild, sublime
but secular enough
to keep the regulars lingering
recognising passion as it strains
to break free of body
bricks and mortar

here's a word I don't understand: lung
breathing big like Sundays
loud, the voice pushing
through the trachea

and something else
I don't understand: the sound
of morning when word came

the acoustics of that finality
butchering the day

writing on leaves

1

this leaf
its diagonal veins
teeming on my tongue

2

not for winter
for summer   to accompany
figs   ripening flames
on the twig

3

in a dark room
the pen punctures
the delicate structure
of death

linear thought
following
oval interpretation

4

the autumn leaf
falls silentleaf

5

with earth

turns caramel

fluttering *imbroglio*

through the forest

6

the leaf   la hoja

      foliage

sayable only

         underfoot

memory

for Sasha Abercorn and Kate Muldoon

deep within these stones
memory runs amuck
in its attempt to speak
         and flow

its accent changes
with our comings and goings
ebbing through the earth
stumbling on the occasional lump
      in its throat
the odd scots or gaelic diphthong
of a pebble colliding
with a blade of grass

we hear it gasp
and stutter in our sleep
though we cannot understand
        a word
rooted as we are in the fixity
of things

the urge to be heard
sweeps the landscape softly
    like a flurry
        lost
the moment it hits the ground

and this is all we have
by way of recollection
this air
        and space
lithographic wisdom now
no more than
whispers
through the waterlines

my opia

in the diagram
the red line A ends abruptly
between
vision and the sky
                    poised
on a transversal plane
trans-genred verse
where understanding should be
located

if it is a measurement of sight
my eye has been reduced
to its curvature
            points in a socket
and I flounder, blindly

following little arrows that point
to links
between the membrane, K
and distance, a radial row
of decimals that are
supposedly
            pieces of pie

mathematical truths crumble
off the edge of my formulae
leaving me

curious

        not about the line

but the space that surrounds it

the unpartnered parenthesis

hurling its contents

into emptiness

(numb-numb)

so much hanging around   to hear or

not to hear from the solicitor

the bank   in the vernacular please

grafted onto my split ends so I can

              cut them off

who are these people   the faceless

plenipotentiaries   I hear them scratching

solemnly behind the skirting boards

       sometimes I see their droppings under the fridge

the laws on harassment leave room for ambiguity

and that's another thing that's not supposed

to be   tolerance / intolerance   hard

to draw a line

      if I had ink I'd pen

95 theses

    too much crooked

    too much mean

    too little cheese to go around and tonight

of all nights is a blue moon   there'll be

denial round the fire   someone laughing

at his own misfortune so hard he'll have

welts on his tongue by morning

fossil statement

the words are bottled
in the brain, waiting
to be burnt to ash
mixed with the humours
that pen the night-scent of ink
cloister each letter
on the page
in careful print

it requires a steady hand
a will as intent
on survival as the trilobite
relying on its shell
for defence, unaware
that its cracks will leave
a fossil statement
for the future

abstract and delicate
the spine slanting
on slate, hinting at
grace of movement
a catalogue of vertebrae
scripted neatly
filling so many tomes
of obsolescence

doing a runner

the girl is invisible   like redwoods
falling
except we don't hear them
can't   questioning the invisible

though she was here
Friday
calling to the door she came and ran away
laughing loo-lah
at the solitary rose that lost its bush   the rose strangled

by the gate   by the sickness of the rope
from which she hung
Tuesday   laughing
at pineapple flowers   the ones that snapple twice a year
on the tree you keep saying is dead

laughing   at the little homey blooms I bought
for their chalky underside   their must-have violet
namelessness   the steady gift of traffic
strutting in the sun   the hum   the ever-presence

she ran away   like those american boys you've been meeting
run   strange how they engage wholeheartedly in combat
but not in conversation
cowboy übermensch – again

              I've never seen them but I believe you –

sterile textbook shoes they walk in
childish humpty walls they build

she came   knocking   because she's not quite through here
not quite laid the quintessential six foot under
a princely depth for her to nestle in
charm the clay   become its shoe tree

not dainty or souffléd   not Hepburn
but hollow burn-eyed   staple-tongued

clay

you've been out again   running
through the ooblek that makes veg
orgasmic   what the american woman
called *shit* with such disgust
her face imploded to half its size   you've
kicked off your sandals so I can feel
the weakness on your foot   this is sabotage

grit and grass   the taste
of come and get me
                    biting fresh into my meat

I'll have to sacrifice myself again
to the nakedness   the fish
and fuck smell of a mortal
and for what?   so you can burn me
over and over and over

gorse

maybe this is it   this peninsular
patch of gorse stretching fingers over the chill

      granite could be the pulse   irregular
up-beats replacing the spire   the shard   gathering
pace down to the sea   yellow swarming for acres
gruff   unshaven   belting
        past the city buzz below

eco everywhere you look   stares back
      lashing your face
         and I don't know if it's a promise
    or the easterlies echoing off my hands
    melting my marrow

I could be frog spawn   untouched by benzene
        or the autism of urban planning
      I could be calatrava's eye

     at this height the air is out of focus   a catalyst
for lungs   new skills   so I sharpen my pencil
    mainly because I'm blind
        and colour is a feeling

let it travel to spaces that invent themselves

as they encounter lead   yellow lead yellow

sienna lemon burnt amber ochre sun

in the tangle of sound swooshing

                              slapsloop

pools where your deeper half can drown

sandwich

the women park themselves
unwrap sunshards, cahoots in tupperware

I pull the cuticle off my thumb
wondering if   when   where the dog
will foul and what his trolling on the grass
says about the gate that has to be pushed
so pulmonary   studiously unclosed unopened

who's to be kept in or out
or just who's to be kept

him being neutered   I'm not sure
what that means though I suspect
it invalidates the path that cuts through
this morning   too early for lunch
too late for soreness   the whiff
of burnt toast skulks round the bench
erected "for mum"   another mystery
until the need to sell up and hunger
elsewhere equally unhinged where
I can get the connections
                    stop the bleeding

sleepless

I'll have the piano tuner
for his fingers   even the one that's
half-missing   inaction
stripping his skin to jazzed-up
       water-wind

Thursday I'll have his face
Friday his tell-tale hair
the strand that lops over his eye
canicular   like summer when the room stings
with his reserve   pitching what he hears
in drum and hammer   coquillage
so pearled and pure I want him to come back

next week   unlock
the spleen in a semitone   petite fleur
swimming from one end of his memory
to my hippocampus   fudged   and back
leaving a wake of structure in the keys
       the spine of residual stars

on my death bed too   I want him
tuning the tunnels from here to all the phantoms
no fanfare   just *pp*   though *agitato*'s ok
       if that's what he wants
we won't be such strangers by then

insomnia

the beauty of pitch
runs aground
turned to banality
of the blackest kind blowing
the night asunder

images invade
brickwall composure
with wordless mortar

dead air
drives a blizzard of thought
through the mind
a wake
for the living

I climb the mattress
the pillow
your hot legs

every pursuit of the house
seconds the creaking

hollow
titanic timbers
about to split
some speaking of ink & depth

of ruin
the ecstasy of other nights

there must be a formula
for this
a physical *s* (sleep)
and *S* (Sheep)
which fall on the wrong side
of the dividing line

nullify the solution
so it bulges imperfectly
equatorial

like these snippits of dusk
volleyed in our chitchat
the nub & crux & soul of it
hurtling off
misfired
outside the confines
of safe conversation

landing
in someone else's dream

Taipei

i wake   my arms wrapped

around the city   legs enjamb-

      ed with its towers

            skyward   /a formal

                           composition/

      silence   /stylized/

        flowers through its lights

the smallness of them   struck

            by shadowed stills

      the colour of cavities

            of not wanting to disturb   /harmony

                          respect/

      28 degrees at midnight   slums unshimmering

slumber   the eye insists on definition

        colour resists   /chaos v order/

            could hang me

        it's a hollow that isn't black

        but marinated

            stinky tofu

        where the street light

                sizzles

maybe it's a smell   a size

        the meaning of a name

             i can never forget   /beautiful

                       soup/

corrugated iron angles into place   discreet   /elegant/

        blanketblue & rustroof red

    staggered across some great want

        where the revolution daubs

    its palette of scars

waiting for Lautrec

I could never and still

cannot not

for lack of trying   I can do the

                    I cccc— ccccccccc—   no

negative   always

it involves me

falling breathless   legs

tree trunks   girders   did you know my coccyx

bends the wrong way as a result   swerves left

          so much contusion

I gave   up   up   (oh, one last time!)   up in the air

but the flourish or gaiety is missing   mostly aardvark again

          in a gym slip   nose

olfactory on the carpet   tubulidentata   good

for ants and mulch out in the middle of nowhere

now… now my joints kick kick scream a bit

starting   and I can even less   there's pain

the body's soliloquy without

grandeur   earth pig   dependent

          on a low centre of gravity

trying to x-ray its way into the secrets

                              of the girls who can

laugh like them   backstage with their legs

          behind their ears

II

at ulica Freta, 16 – before radium or polonium

the wood seeps into your bones
in a room that lives   as if its grain
& whorls were part of your nervous
system – smooth marrow – polished

in your tea one lump, two   meticulous
the molecules contract till they disappear
            optical illusions have their own reality

billowing on the balcony Poland
is diluted   Prussian Russian
fission renames a people
            invents a purpose of its own

but you can shut it out   indomitable
in a room that soon is rubble while thunder
splits the summer   partitions your
future   gladioli everywhere   alert
to your black dress   alive   your luggage
                waltzing in the street

armchair traveller

the traveller gets weary of sitting
on a mosaic of dreams
rooted in jaw-dropping green

leaves beckon   emeralds and sunsets call
the hope of meeting a tartar
        or personal dragoman

his scream is loud enough to worry his mother
                for real

after so many (dis)illusions
the house becomes a blanket   grey

his head fills with rotting rafters   kitchen clatter
dank holes gaping   and the old comforts even become
          inspirational

he could dig a small channel
        from the chair to the table
        might be enough
sail across it   pack his trunk with the names
of exotic places
        Belmullet   Clonturk

he could board a steamer
    watch the ripples dapple lapis

malin jade   sex black   sucking him

into ribboned reflections that tie him to home

the bow claiming him   amorphous

colourless   for its own abstractions

no man's land

in the back of the car
splicing pipas through Quijote country
we watch the bull loom black
on hills that take half a day to arrive

our bickering is what turns
those sunflowers heads, cramped
in fell after field like us sardines

they spit us out – husk and tumbleweed
across the set for spaghetti westerns
neither here nor there
the bull a shadow propped high

this is all the world there is
Osborne, king of the dust and boredom
his armature a proper coat of arms
proper logo in the wind milling round us

where is Jerez, anyway, or what
and how can so many worlds be earthed
in no man's land
that bull the toro bó Cuailgne charging
charging
its balls in our blood

horoscopes

horoscopes remind me
that I'm intra-venus and unstable
descendant of various houses
that were demolished
crushed before I curlicued to flesh
and flushed to life

the ruins are abstract
rooms no more than cells
globules dimorhping through veins

capillaries pump and prance
questioning the statelet status of canals
nautilus v. island, brittle

                      as venetian glass

couched on flagstone prati
I constellate, buck&bronco bridges
over steeples to my getaway

bull by the horns for breakfast
carry me
corrupt me
crave me cornucopian, bird's-eye
round the moon, its rings
its faceless hado

lines from *The Irish Times*

I hate saying it but we are where we are

devastated numbday

concerning the obvious inflation, above the 3% limit and underneath

every single one of those rooftops is a horror story

trials, indifference

to trials

the two fingers

some absolutely love it, immune from the application of the law

It is unjust

the warnings are of danger, loss of biodiveristy

perhaps more surprising is the presence of Fight Like Apes

popular obsessions with the weather, potholes, fantastic electrofolk stylings

a real shame that the Solar Bears haven't been recognised

fun, amuse, inform keystones to pedagogy—you might like to demonstrate
        to children some of the properties of water

though you've difficulty making an emotional connection

stressed for three solid years and need to stop

what makes someone a kind, warm person tapping into and beyond our
        greatest hopes

amazing

the doctor said all this about her

but

but

there is outrage at a man and a woman who appear to be on the verge
        of a kiss

paranoia—if you're not with us you're against us

"I order the defendant be held to answer" – he sounded nervous

Hedda Gabler, vulgar and hedonistic, outside the courthouse

we could draw strength from one another, appear pleased at the outcome

appear Randy

bridling at the suggestion that we are less than forthcoming

but

there is deep anger and a feeling of helplessness

fear of the future

fudge at the fissures and a profound sense of betrayal

there is, to a worrying degree, disillusionment

inconvenience caused to householders and the business community

but

having a hissy fit about a hoe is a peculiarly dispiriting, undignified,
       experience

giving rise to damages for Post Traumatic Stress Disorder

depressive disorder

nervous shock

nightmares

bewildering

feet foot-working the concrete on their busy
busy way through streets
legging it A to B under cctv against the clock around
the clock around the bus, the tram, the man
who's sitting half-bridged across
a river of piss, home
with his cardboard box and his sign
quietly colouring your trajectory
as he sinks into asphalt
– beggars
belief –

but forget compassion, you don't
have time and it's unsavoury under section 2
of the Criminal Offences (Public
Order) Act 2011, Acts of kindness
or generosity must not be encouraged, must not be
seen
they foment
disorder, social dyspepsia
unlike potholes, back-handers, tv screens
harassing you at every supermarket checkout

the law is hissing seductively in your pocket
curled round your hand, steering you through the city
like a good committee to protect you from
the gutter, the guts
of puked proposals, quangos, soiled reports
it might all be too real, too toxic for your delicate
entrails, it might cause a random thought to break and enter
into your head, rewire
a moment of consciousness, conscience
that could lay the roots
of revolt, separate you
from the health and safety
of the herd

elegy

the world is standing still
stunned behind a dislocated
door
        open it
and the room is flooded
with emptiness
mental oil spill

countries mapped like crumbs
across a plate
easily devoured
I lick congo from my fingers
       and an elephant
gets caught between
my teeth

pick pick pick ivory
abuse, amnesia, pick
the mine of children silent
in my mouth
regurgitating gold and diamonds
stripping sunsets
by the bloated
           bellyful
the famished
guts of slavery

I lick malawi
and ornichognathus walleri
sings
     or not
            perched
on the bars of a cloud
of toxins
terror stuck in its throat

Manhal

here is Manhal – not his real name –
his real name is mangled
      under the rubber of a boot
at his jaw   his fingers less righteous than yours
dripping blood   unable to point

his ear's split   electrodes pinned
      to the quiet parts of his protest
till he hears his skin through the surge
singeing the seconds   then minutes
     a scream which may not even be his

another day is kicked out of his mouth
relentless it burns to ash in the dark
      with butts that have branded his feet
lacerates its way to print in a world that is
a lifetime away   Manhal aged thirteen
paying for belief   things you cannot touch
         or see

time blurs   smouldering in his head   time
that has come too soon   too late   spring
in disguise   summer in revolt   and death
     death in strobes   physical as the boy
standing in the street last week   speaking a tongue
now tied to despair   now swelling with the crowd
     its news contused   outraged

take me by the foot

take me by the foot
unravel me
wrap yourself

in spirals round my leg
measuring muscle tone
unshaven hair

you could carve
your crimes
on my thigh, those dreams

of piracy brushing
curls of pubic coastline
and I wouldn't tell

as long as it was
a story good enough
to bury deep inside me

treasure hidden
with the sweat of flesh
on flesh, rhythm

dripping over me
echoing
in the cavity of your chest

taking steps

one step
leads to another
squelch of mud

I've left the beaten track
left tarmac
for the surprise
of an appoggiatura up a tree

my destination:
deliberate surrender
to a sound, a somewhere
that places me
inside-out

I manoeuvre my foot carefully
on a cloud
of silt and sink
underground into the forest

maybe I've just trodden
on a song
flattened an iridescence
with my clumsy boot
the celesta tinkling
as it flits across my line of sight

echoes

i

year's end and we've all grown

thin   dodging gloss in the streets

      and you choose your path guided only

by the dry patch

      the way you chose your toys   once

          by quirk

ii

ahead of you is the splash you tried so hard

to avoid   a slough of limited responses

      someone shouts your name

but you've no idea what to say   it's probably

      not even you   your tongue

keeps chaffing off chipped teeth   pearls

      in need of tracks

iii

      comfort is a thing

of the past   to behold   forget perhaps

now all you ask is a shelf to curl up on   the offer

          of closure

    or a kick-start   buttons to press so at least

your fingers are employed

Pichincha

the anniversary meal

was a sandwich

impossible to quantify   I would say

                     you take my breath away

as we chew on cheese and high   high
on the view   decreased oxygen

                    levels

                    us

also making pronouncements that have

                        something to do

                                  with love

elevating it   to dizziness   vertigo

it's too much for me
this splendour that reduces everything to nothing

           the summit
           telluric
           out of reach

my head in its cloud

leaving Cobh

you hold me
in the palm of your hands
my vision snaking
out to sea

          up

         down

    the waves
as I hoist a sail as I
      unravel youth

        the ropes
tingle with preparatory songs
untangle the wind in my paper boat

children poke and cradle me
see me off
     away !
       with a curious kiss
of ice-cream and cliffs
            curl like your fingers
       round me

the idea of terra firma was pulverised
long ago
by those mountains of ocean
    beckoning
each wave

confirming the need to

                           climb

             fall

       hurt

embrace the dangers

beyond the band stand

and St. Coleman's chiming

tidal in my ear

the need to plunder

                  the edge

      of the pier

fathom the thin line between

      leaving

      and

      losing my mind

I imagine this is where

the piracy begins

where you hold me captive

to your sorrows

scrubbing ancestral memory

from the deck

while the world sneaks illegal substances

into my dreams

      a gram of doubt or fear

I beat and tack across

your steady palms, thinking

                    your breath
is a favourable wind
thinking there's some exotic
elsewhere marked
                    X
on a map I might yet find

III

playing messiaen

for Thérèse Fahy

Birdsong rushes morning
to the tips of her fingers
quivering through trapezium
tapping from the trapezoid
capitulating to the capitate
the hammering of hamate

how to trap a sound –
bend its bones to breaking
tame the thrush in the hand
            worth two nightingales
            still chirping in the bush
subdue through orchestration
deft manipulation
in order to rework, replay, release

through honey-handed practice
practice practice practice
as the distal pecks and pokes
repeating keys it hones
plinks furthest from the body
soft loud piano *forte*
twitter soft
            tweet!
the bird, the hand, the ear
and bated breath
hunger for a habitat
worming through the piano jaw
trilling in a language that rebels

against all time and meter hour
and season till it

        stops!

a   noon   cloud   sneaks   by
      silence   rubs   itself   raw

far   away   the   bark
          of   a   birch

silver leaves sucking light seeking sun
cortex heaves at the woodpecker's
rat-a-tat-a-tat
implodes under the weight
of a sound sent to
        attack
siege by castanet, celeste
the birds are at her peck and call
as she modulates the pitch
stuffs the staves with sonic shifts
lunges into biorhythms, microtones
rush and gush of arabesques
the foot all furious action
timbre tumbling from the lark
harking back to desert bush
the nest packed tight and then
the jagged *crack* of birth
a song to celebrate the egg
jackdaw chack-chack-chacking

chaffinch chaffing skin
that swoops and glides
and rubs and races
fingers camouflaged as feathers
as they flutter, speckled, cheeeky
crested, fly, choke the spaces
in between the sounds

not

a

sound

messiaen messing with me here
messing with my ear, harnessing
some harsh realities – the tongue
is - not - a - tune   the hand - is - not
a - hum, they are lumpish lunate
muscle melody impeccably performed
true to form, and to intent
but lunacy
            falling short
                      of truth

supress the metacarpal metaphor
take a break.
go for a walk
                  in the woods

burn the energy of stillness
on your retina
the intervals of whispering
the speed of savage
on your scaphoid,

listen to the phrase that cannot
be controlled even when you hold it
in the palm of your hand
it's just a moood
to move you – no more
a caging of the senses, ineffable
approximation of a freedom

like a la-la-la-la-laugh
impossible to trap

Birds sing microtones. They phrase in arabesques that swoop and glide.

Their staccato "notes" are more like jagged shards than human musicians' points
and beads of sound. The timbres and attacks are often energetic to the point of
harshness, yet to our ears in the wild they may sound ineffably sweet.
(http://ccrma.stanford.edu/courses/220a-fall-2003/sep-30.html)

Birdsong moves faster than human fingers

Nightingale
Little Owl
Wryneck
Cetti's Warbler
Wood Lark
Blackbird
Nightjar
Chiffchaff
Robin
Song Thrush
Chaffinch
Mistle Thrush

Whitethroat

Cuckoo

Great Spotted Woodpecker

Melodious Warbler

Hoopoe

Green Woodpecker

Hedge Sparrow

House Sparrow

Redstart

Golden Oriole

Carrion Crow

Magpie

Blackcap

Turtle Dove

Blue Tit

Linnet

Wren

Garden Warbler

Willow Warbler

Greenfinch

Serin

Nuthatch

Goldfinch

Starling

Bonelli's Warbler

Wood Pigeon

- 1. scaphoid
- 2. lunate
- 3. triquetrum
- 4. pisiform
- 5. trapezium
- 6. trapezoid

- 7. capitate
- 8. hamate

the end of time
in the distal
distance ringing
ringing

what sound does a leaf make
what language does a feather speak

all wrapped in pjs   we are as if strapped

to ourselves   camouflaged   not daring to breathe

among seventies fibres   carpet that looked

insensitive   felt like grass but was not

harbouring battles up   up the steps to where

secretly the children -us- struggle for sound for a glimpse

through the banisters   of adults perfumed

at the front door being led   following

          bleating into the dining room

                              evenings of polite

politicking over pork   apple sauce was glamorous then

          a glimpse not of the adults but us   futuro-fat

guests in our own fiction wondering

          who/what are you or will you be?

pink rinse with long cigar   fossilized codger

saying the child is impish seen AND heard

          not silenced like now   adult   falling off

the leg of the spider diagram into inequities

insolvencies   sludgemire unsolved erasing the innocence

on those faces that were us peeking from quicksand

                              before the sandman

          what did we expect   no   really

                    what

high-wire

after César Vallejo

what is the moment
suspended on a geometry of emotion –
the line between this
         and that
now
   and then
supporting the weight of the walker
one foot rising
cajoling oxygen, hydrogen
the nitric toe
searching blindly for the tension
as vision vibrates

seeing is as useless
as knowing the angles
distances
there is no comfort
in calculation

the foot relies on other armour
on the breath
a balance of spirit
that translates three meters
into applause

the taut rapture of spectacle

and belief, belief

always beyond the physical

the moment is performed

years in advance

long before the foot

has learned to dream

on first reading Stuart Kendall's *Gilgamesh*

spasms   because
you move the maenad in me[1]

        tongue
     between your toes
     slow curl under
        paleolithic suck

these garments in the later paintings   wispy
veils and want-want weave   are too
        dreary
    dead as sleep in Nineveh[2]

     I've ripped them up   gauzy arabesque
of the type you imagined
     in your weaker moments
           might be
      pulled off a shoulder
      teased away to please
             reveal...

            y aaaaa wn

            my mouth
            cannot
            be naked
            any
            wider

i'm off to ride the bull   if not slay it
    before hunting your gods

           who said love is like a red red[3] rose...

---

[1] we can make this
        tomorrow's fetish   we must
[2] http://en.wikipedia.org/wiki/Nineveh
[3] so clichéd   and Neruda's poetry is over-rated too

it is
and there's the rub

we need a good secateurs

I digress   the real garment
is not wispy gauze but woven with my pubic hair[4]
          the primitive joy of it
          against your thighs and your crotch

          your hands chained
          behind the chair

               it's woven to the crenellations
               where we left the castle tour
               to rewrite the untouched histories
               of nooks   hidden places[5]

               where we could be
               mythical   animal
               where *cunt* and *prick* and *fuck*
               are not pejorative

the silken milk-and-honey bollocks
in the later paintings of the maenads
          burns the painter's brush

          their buttocks is worthy of more
                              more realism
          rubbing off Bacchus' godly stubble
          proper burlap chin   rubble upper lip
                    red red real[6]

---

[4] Bethesda
houses your civility   healing
                    is irrelevant after this
[5] in full view
[6] / love doesn't come into it

their juices[7] dripping lava over his face
      melting his tongue

their lungs a feckless howl[8]   shredding sheets
        the way storms strip
        the sky
        deflower
        the forest

---

[7] is there another word for that?
[8] think Ginsberg

Utopia

for Olivier Cornet – after a painting by Jordi Forniés

in every fleck a reverie
unfurls the weave, each world
stacked as codex silk and spice
kaleidoscopic in our field
of vision   the best days

are the days that poppy pulse
and sing, read like saffron sutras
devil's helmet rampant through our hair

days that bring the ancestry of grain
like rain again in lapis runnels
scattered by the mothers of invention
then caramel the chaff
of wheat   pearl and eggshell flour
the women's fingers working
stone on stone   giving birth to bread

stories leven

                    in the kilim and it breathes
monsoon   sirocco   speaks
in equinox dancing elfin blue on surpar
and the terraces of ancient wonder are sutured
deep in memory   layer on layer
of turquoise, malachite, stanching
loss with orchids, mango sun, gamboge

the lore is mustard-seed and scrolls

coptic westward-bound wrapped

in honeycomb and zeal

its gods and demons

cloistered on the palette   the best days

are the days that script their steps

in wonder   thrill us sandalwood

to our forgotten selves, not of these parts

peony   madder   impermanence

a fleck of jasper in the peacock's tail

        a mote of dust

Jezebel

no   i can't say

anything about that   *wither my fingers*

                                       as the hazel branch

                           burn my eyes

                           be i smitten   *be i hurled*

                           by his brothers and his sisters

                                       from my window to my death

i can't say the marriage fell apart

round about the time

i stopped doing his ironing

round about the time i stopped

round about the time for breaking bread

when fear black blossomed

and his mother's spittle and his sister's spite

soured on my face

                           fustigate me desert winds!

                        be i accursed   *bludgeoned*   *poxed*

i can't say that i fell

fell for the wrong person

                     made the wrong choice

                    falling is predestined

i have only myself to blame that he lacked
vision to see my loyalty

i can't say
falling hurts   *struck be i*   *incinerated*   *and my tongue*
                                        timely plucked by demons

falling for the wrong person
is allowed
only sometimes
when falling
works to his advantage
when his advantage is to hold all the cards
he the king

although   *miserable i*

                                        castigate and chasten me!

it probably requires some ironing too
and sex
        the deep abyss of silence
        that surrounds the sex of the abused

        i can't say
the circumstances

my ears be hacked   *thwart my thoughts!*

but sex is a good bargaining chip

tell that to your daughters   at least

i can't say anything about sex

            because it's unsavoury   he says

            and if he says so then [   ]

                              balsam for his ears !

there's a tussle over that

tussle   a euphemism for battery that goes unreported

i can't say that either

                        BAAL I beseech you !

i can't say that i worked hard to build our home

that i toiled to bear our children

that all my labours were for them

i can't say that i sacrificed myself

because the woman who works too hard

concerns herself with the material

is jezebel   far from home

            scorned maligned

the material must only be a man

who stitches a woman's lips

holds the privilege of provision

working too hard

is only allowed

when working too hard

works out

         there are questions surrounding this

         that i must not ask   not now

                              not then

       patience

              then chastity

              temperance

              charity

              diligence

              kindness

              humility

      i have been a virtuous wife

                             smite me!

                             vented be their wrath

                             wind-whipped on my skin

i can't say

i sold myself short

because i sold nothing

      all i had were the chirpful mornings of my youth

      a fickle fate

and trust   which i freely gave

as if all adventures in trust

were for the taking

to be pillaged

> *hack my limbs!   a plague descend on me!*
>
> > *i am dust under his feet*
> >
> > > *and the feet of my sons*

> *cast me to the ground   my flesh*
>
> > *be ripped by dogs!*

i can say none of this

because there is no evidence

> (they will think me mad)

it is only what i know in my heart

it is my life

> every minute and every hour of the life i built
>
> > on sand

the dead

always with us

the dead

engulf the waking hours   the could have been

                                        that never was

                                        that is

                    el cielo está entaravintintangulado

                    ¿quién lo desentantaravintintangulará?

narrative interrupted like prayers I've forgotten

and somewhere sepia my foot is still

                small enough to fit your hand

back when the night was jasmine and the crickets epic

                el cid

                casilda

                juana la loca

the dead   voiced for bed-time

                within arm's reach

dirge and myth in the dingy room

magicking your mouth

                                my ears

                                          the barking dogs

el desentantaravintintangulador que lo desentantaravintintangule
¡buen desentantaravintintangulador será!

stars ripe as figs ghost the way home

peeled the proper way   with your pen-knife

pith north of my lips
                    astrolabial

we'll never be lost – remember –
now you're dead
            and I hold your life
                      your kith
                    and flint

Acknowledgements

The author would like to thank the following publications where some of these poems first appeared:

And Agamemnon Dead, Can-Can, Formafluens, Osiris, Penduline, Poethead, Poetry Ireland, Poetry Salzburg Review, Seven Towers' *Census* Anthology, *Shearsman, The Stony Thursday Book, Tears in the Fence, Upstart.*

On a more personal note, I am very grateful to Kit Fryatt for inspiring some of the poems with her energetic Wurm im Apfel readings in Dublin; to Paul Casey, founder of Ó Bhéal in Cork, for showing me around Cobh where one particular statue led to the poem 'Leaving Cobh'; to the late Sarah Lundberg, founder of the Seven Towers Last Wednesday reading series in Dublin – renamed The Sunflower Sessions – which for many years has been an invaluable testing ground for fledgling poems; to Jennifer Matthews for her inspiration while we worked towards a collaborative collection that succumbed to greater forces, but which resulted in several of the poems included here; to Tony Frazer of Shearsman for supporting my work and for his tireless commitment to poetry in translation.

www.ingramcontent.com/pod-product-compliance
Lightning Source LLC
Chambersburg PA
CBHW022201080426

42734CB00006B/538